Coloring Book for Adults
World Series: Europe

Coloring Book for Adults

WORLD SERIES: EUROPE

Amsterdam

NETHERLANDS

Andorra La Vella

ANDORRA

Athens

GREECE

Belgrade

SERBIA

Berlin

GERMANY

Bern

SWITZERLAND

Bratisla a

SLOVAKIA

Brussels

BELGIUM

Budapest

HUNGARY

Bucharest

ROMANIA

Chisinau

MOLDOVA

Copenhagen

DENMARK

Dublin

IRELAND

Helsinki

FINLAND

Istanbul

TURKEY

Kyi

UKRAINE

Lissabon

PORTUGAL

Ljubljana

SLOVENIA

London

ENGLAND

Luxembourg

LUXEMBOURG

Madrid

SPAIN

Minsk

BELARUS

Monaco

PRINCIPALITY OF MONACO

Moscow

RUSSIA

Nicosia

REPUBLIC OF CYPRUS

Oslo

NORWAY

Paris

FRANCE

Podgorica

MONTENEGRO

Prague

CZECH REPUBLIC

Reykjavik

ICELAND

Riga

LATVIA

Rome

ITALY

City of San Marino

REPUBLIC OF SAN MARINO

Sarajevo

BOSNIA AND HERZEGOVINA

Skopje

NORTH MACEDONIA

Sofia

BULGARIA

Stockholm

SWEDEN

Tallinn

ESTONIA

Tirana

ALBANIA

Vaduz

LIECHTENSTEIN

Valletta

MALTA

Vatican City

VATICAN CITY STATE

Vienna

AUSTRIA

Vilnius

LITHUANIA

Warsaw

POLAND

Zagreb

CROATIA

Printed in France by Amazon
Brétigny-sur-Orge, FR